POETIC SWORDZ

CURTIS GUY

POETIC SWORDZ

0-9554732-0-9
978-0-9554732-0-3

First Published December 2006
BAD BREED BOOKS

Printed in Great Britain for BAD BREED BOOKS

POETIC SWORDZ

Dedicated to my son in New York,
Far away but always in my heart.

And to all the youths on road.

ACKNOWLEDGEMENTS

First of all a massive thanks to the Most High Almighty, then I want to say a big thank you to my woman Lorraine for believing in my work and inspiring me to write this book. A big thanks to Rachel Celia for your help in my life, then I want to send love to Jermaine, Shanay, Keiron, Ashley, Jayden and the rest of my family, Dad (RIP) Mum, Uncle Donald, Aunty Barbara, Bernadette, Harry, Basil, Leonard, Navelette, Agnes, Wendell, Nadine, Keiron, Stephan, Justine, Julian, Chelsey, Davina, Christina, Rosie and all my other cousins in Reading.

A big shout to Jason, Kenneth, Mikey Phillips, Derek, Mark, Leon, Gary, Mark (from the Bridge) Andrea, Collis, Michelle, Dionne, Otis. Suzette, Angie and Colin (Bean).

Preview

This book will take you on a poetical journey through life in today's society. Many of us especially black people, seem to be sleepwalking aimlessly through life, abandoning the morals our parents raised us on and falling victim to all the bullshit that the government and media has been feeding us on.

More concerned about the next bag of weed, and buying designer clothes than marching against injustice or maybe gun crime, but soon as you mention rave, we're sure to come out in numbers.

Look at the youths, misguided and out of control running the streets, but who created them? Did we take time to nurture them and guide them through this society, where it is ok for two man to join like husband and wife, where its cool to dress your young daughter like a big woman, and video games that teach our kids extreme violence and even murder.

The world is moving so fast, but sometimes we need to slow down and revaluate our environment, check ourselves and our children. So many fatherless youths and worthless so-called fathers, to selfish to even take time out for them.

I could go on forever, but I won't, just read this book, enjoy and keep your minds open.

Keep It Real!

*Curtis Guy (*AUTHOR)

CONTENTS

56. Lets Pray

GOVERNMENT SLAVE

As the sun sets to mark the end of the day
I wipe my brow and sigh,
Was we born from the womb with these debts to pay?
Then mother please tell me why,
We wake at dawn to the sound of birds
But do you listen to their song?
Is it a song of joy or imprisoned words?
The fruits of the land have gone

Shackled by these unseen chains
Seldom do we reap from our labour,
Enduring physical and emotional strains
With only hope to savour,
Wealthy men will cling to possessions
The humble man is rich in mind,
For life is a road of signs and lessons
The road to wisdom with must find

Only then can we see the true horizon
And walk side by side with the brave,
Is this our existence?
Merely a government slave.

BLACK WOMAN

Made with masterful hands
You were created to perfection,
The natural beauty of the land
An image of your own reflection

Man will stop you in your path
Undress you within their minds,
Fail to see that woman of class
A cloud of lust has made them blind

Your body is a spiritual place
The wise see you as a queen,
Only with your king you embrace
An satisfy your wildest dreams

Still you're degraded by fools
Do they not know who you are?
They chase diamonds and miss the real jewels
That strong black woman who came from far.

THE GUN AND THE DARKNESS

Darkness all around unfolds
Shadows hide beneath hoods,
Mindless fools with hearts so cold
Faces set like they were carved from wood

Introduce that icy steel
The devils tool for power,
With a loaded chamber equipped to kill
A young blood lives his final hour

Darkness is inside our homes
Hidden in games our children play,
Fathers fail to guide their own
While lost men lead our kids astray

They verse words of material gain
The streets they left are crying,
Glorifying the gangster game
"Get rich or die trying"

Darkness in higher places
They plot to suffer millions,
The stress of life on people's faces
On the streets innocent civilians

Gunshots heard for many miles
Another night of bloodshed
A mother waits for her child
Uniformed men confirm he's dead.

REMEMBER

The sun seemed to shine different
So innocent when we played,
Warmth was all around us
Life we had if made

With picky heads and trousers swinging
And shirts that look like planes,
Trying hard to impress the girls
Feeling sweet in the latest names

Sundays were so peaceful
Just neighbours washing cars,
Mr Patel grinning in his shop
English men propping up the bars

Pastor Money in his church
Preaching brimstone and fire,
Tambourines filling the place with noise
Afros swaying in the choir

Remember that sweet soul music
Those songs that came from the heart,
So much love was in them tunes
Singers who truly new their art

Them old time reggae beats
Your Uncle doing the one foot skank,
Gregory bursting through the speakers
Strong rum flowing in the tank

Playing knock down ginger
Days of hide and seek,
Coming home late from school
Those licks we used to reap.

Long old school holidays
When we longed for September,
Memories of way back then
Too many for me to remember

Me in 1976 (Life was simple)

The 70's (The Good Days)

ROCKS

My street name is Rocks
They call my father Cocaine,
I run estates and control blocks
The master of my domain

Don't be deceived by my size
For my power is immense,
Even the hardest of men have fallen
Mesmerized by my strength

The badman of the streets
Government know me well,
Bred me through my father
Sent to bring you hell

I am the author of deceit
The Jack of all trades
Murder lies and riches
The filler of many graves

My street name is Rocks
They call my father Cocaine,
I run estates and control blocks
The master of my domain

Your wife I'll enslave
Take beauty from her face,
Watch her degrade herself
For me she'll long to taste

Desperation by your side
And me your closest friend,
A tunnel full of darkness
You'll long to see the end

Wishing you never knew me
Others may have that choice,
For now I have revealed myself
My name is Rocks, hear my voice

My street name is Rocks
They call my father Cocaine,
I run estates and control blocks
The master of my domain.

SUPERNATURAL

Supernatural that's what you are
Mother of the land,
With that baby girl you've come so far
You've raised that little man

Blessed so that you could bring forth life
The first seed was sown,
Into the world grasping for air
The greatest pain you ever known

Like a lioness guarding her pride
You watch them grow and learn,
Daddy out in the wilderness
Lost and unlikely to return

Cowardly he runs through concrete jungles
Leaving you to fend,
Made with strength you never crumble
On you they will depend

From the time they left the womb
And suckled on your breast,
The bond between mother and child
A queen ruling her nest

Sometimes you feel disheartened
Your patience often strained,
Showered with pains of motherhood
Still you struggle through the rain

Forget that fool who failed you
Wasn't there to hear their cries,
The strongest woman in the world
Seen through their young eyes

Supernatural that's what you are
Mother of the land,
With that little girl you've come so far
You've raised that little man.

PLASTIC THUGS

They're everywhere these plastic thugs
Like shadows in the mist,
Missing true identity
Just trying to exist

Mass produced like action figures
Never quite made the grade,
Comfortable among their own
Blind to see their being played

Designers use them like puppets
Rap music helped them switch,
I see dead men walking
No education trying to get rich

Blocked by walls of ignorance
In bred self destruction,
Playing out that gangster role
Like a movie in production

Guns have become their armour
Violence now the norm,
Society has them programmed
They comply and perform

Murdering images of themselves
Like soldiers on the streets,
Just like follow my leader
I sit and watch the sheep

Fathers gave no direction
No destiny on the table,
Wanting to be different
Scared to remove the label

They're everywhere these plastic thugs
Like shadows in the mist
Missing true identity
Just trying to exist.

MURDERER

How can you take life?
When you do not have the power
To blow new breath

Who gave you the right?
When to decide
To turn life into death

IN A LAND...

In a land built from slavery
In a land where black people died
In a land that did not see their bravery
In a land they were crucified

Blacks were among the pilots
In their armies fought with vengeance,
Often on the frontline
Never mentioned on remembrance

In a land where we express our views
In a land that does not listen
In a land where our news is no news
In a land of television

Our heroes and inventors
Left out of the hall of fame,
No mark of our achievements
Unless we are winning gold in games

In a land where justice does not prevail
In a land so pure and white
In land where black men die in cells
In a land of equal rights

Brainwash education
The truth tainted with lies,
A month of recognition
For the history of our lives

In a land of many nations
In a land where history's hidden
In a land where we're kept from the truth
In a land called Great Britain.

NAH COOK! WON'T COOK

Two large pizza fe de whole ah dem
Da cooker lose him slave,
Nobody nah cook again
Me Granmudder turning in her grave

Wha happen to da days of old
When we did cook food pon Sunday,
Wait til that pot got cold
And warm it up again pon Monday

Now we get so westernised
No need fe kitchen knife,
Everyting dun cook and curry
Da microwave become we wife

Nah cook! Won't cook!
Good food used to sweet
Nah cook! Won't cook!
Ah wah we ago eat?

Onion crying in the fridge
Long fe see da pot,
Peppersauce jus can't believe
How ketchup tek him spot

Hard food gone back a yard
The Colonel shop get rush,
Coated then Kentucky fried
Wid secret spice him teef from us

Ask the kids bout proper food
Dem tell you Macky D's,
Look how dem fat and have no use
Never seen no rice and peas

Nah cook! Won't cook
Good food used to sweet,
Nah cook Won't cook
Ah wah we ago eat?

INVISIBLE MAN

When did they last see you?
You disappeared
Like magic,
Unseen
Just an old picture,
Shameful
Tragic

You sleep so peaceful
They toss and turn,
Thinking of dad
A father they have never had,
No concern!

Your existence
A fragment of their imagination,
Weak describes you
A boy,
Fatherhood a situation

The power to disappear
But no hero,
Your seeds misguided
Selfish
That's you less than zero,
Vanished
Like a man on quick sand,
They wait patiently
For you
The Invisible Man.

FEDZ

I am a criminal before I even committed a crime
Uneducated before I speak,
This is my ride
Look at my hands full of blisters
Working hard all week

You want to lock me up
When I am free
I don't belong in cells,
Prison is no place for me
My soul wants to rebel

My heart skips when I see you
Even though I am innocent,
I am walking fully legal
Your ways makes no sense
You lack the understanding of equal

How did I assault you?
When handcuffs bound my wrists,
You swear on the bible
Lie in courts
No arrest did I resist

Stop and search my inner space
Do I look like I am packing?
Have a blade on my person,
The streets are just a road to me
But they won't believe my version.

THE DEATH OF RAP

This is the grave of Rap
Who died an untimely death,
Artist's used and abused her
To spit venom through every breath

The streets she reunited
We celebrate her birth,
No place for guns and blades
Peaceful battles took place through verse

Rap became a phenomenon
Through hip hop she reigned,
Followers used her deeply
Perpetrators entered the game

Rapidly Rap was tainted
Gangster made his entrance,
Tricked her into a contract
To use nigga in every sentence

The promoters loved Gangsters style
Made Gangster and Rap join force,
Eventually they captured the world
With no signs of divorce

They came from every coast
Violently they spread the word,
Only a few stayed faithful to Rap
Beneath the noise they were barely heard

The youths were soon captivated
For Gangster they had passion,
They emulated his every move
And followed in his fashion

Rap no longer dignified
Her sisters turned to Ho's,
Gangster loses his art form
The industry still grows

More murder music's played
Raps' to week to stay,
Gangster and his clones get rich
Silently she passes away.

SNAKE

Belly down in the grass
Envious eyes
Blending in with the green
I saw you when I passed,
You could have joined me
But you stayed slippery

Losing focus
Hissing behind my back
Plaguing me like locus,
I worked hard for my cake
Jealously consumes you
I see you snake
I see you.

CRIMINAL JUSTICE

Is it justice for the criminal?
Is the criminal now the victim?
If this is the system
Then the systems looking grim,
Jailbirds fly from prison gates
Sentences cut short
Freed from captivity
No justice in the court

Victims left to pay the cost
Judges controversial,
Injustice now universal
Who will carry the cross?
Cold-blooded murderers
Walking free
Ashes to ashes, dust to dust
While the killers dwell among us

Miles and miles of prison files
Among them paedophiles,
Given grace, how twisted
I'd watch that judge around your child,
Petty thief inside your home
Don't breach his human rights,
His rights to take what you own
No rights for you to fight,
Criminal Justice!

BEDROOM BADMAN

Ah you da Bedroom Badman
Da true lady killer,
Ah you de girls dem wan
Enter the bedroom thriller

Da girls dem sugar
Cruise da Black Starliner,
Woman stop you inna ya path
Dress up inner designer

Run dem through da sheets
Mek dem body shiver,
You alone can rock dem boat
Sail dem pon de river

Gal from every borough
Gal from city gal from town,
Ah you ah run dem thorough
None ah dem Badman nah turn down

Coulda hol ah wifey
A gal fe love and cherish,
Badman catch up inna disease
Life soon done and perish

Ah you da Bedroom Badman
Now you catch the killer,
Badman get what him wan
Fe star inna de bedroom thriller.

POLITICS

Scrolls and scripts
Political tricks
More talk on law and order,
Unrest in the Middle East
No control of the borders

Parties in the Parliament
Wages hardly spent,
Fire in our pockets
Burning away our pounds and pence,
Taxing innovations
Holding us to ransom,
Prisoners in this free world
Politicians sitting handsome

Suffer the children watch them perish
They call it The Third World,
How true a word
Because war comes first
Everything else is second
And Africa is always third.

JUST FOR THE TEMPLE

The smoothest brothers like gallant knights
Roaming through terrain,
Looking unsuspecting Princesses
For them to conquer and tame,
Words flowing from silky tongues
Voices so sentimental,
Seducing their undeveloped minds
To get inside the temple

Promises of sweet romance
Young girl so naïve,
Men well versed in the birds and bees
No control of underneath,
Wedding vows are hidden
The wife kept confidential,
A man on a mission
To get inside the temple

Like a modern day Jekyll and Hyde
The face of a Prince,
Breezed through like a thief in the night
She hasn't seen him since,
Carrying baby and all alone
So young with potential,
Disillusioned by his moves
To get inside the temple.

RAP STAR

These young men are watching you
You fit their idea of a role model,
Who else are they going to follow?
Those two fools on Eastenders
Or Sir Trevor Mc Donald

Where's the empowerment?
When now we're all niggas
Sold your soul
For the cheapest price
Just to turn those records into figures

Now you're flossing your riches
But where's the depth to your cause?
The ghetto suffering
We're self destructing,
But its ok, cos you've got yours.

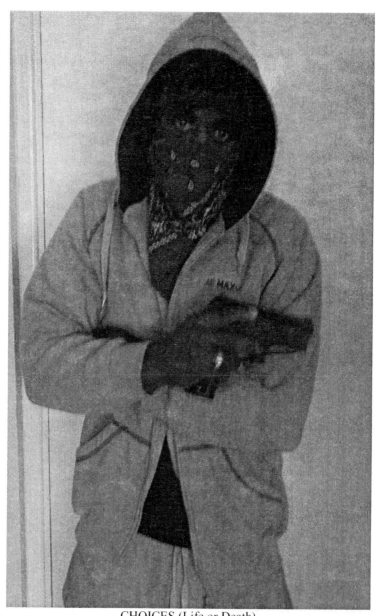

CHOICES (Life or Death)

COCK BACK N CLICK

The sweats pouring from me
I am face to face with dilemma,
My street cred is in tatters
Dilemma wants me to deal with the matter

I'm here now
The road seems dusty,
Moonlight appears to have me in the spotlight
Holding death in my hands ever so tight,
Getting hit with split second thoughts

My body is shaking with momentum
A mixture of nerves and anguish,
I see my bredrins take life before me
Do they have no conscience?
They must do, surely

Fighting to steady the piece
The cold metal resting inside my palms,
Poised on the trigger ready to squeeze
He didn't speak, but his eyes are begging me
Please!

I see flashes of his family mourning
Pain ripping through his mothers' side,
His children playing with no father
I see our two lives collide,
I watch him he's young and black
Just like me,
Shall I put it back?
Or shall I cock back n click?

DA REAL TERRORIST

Ah who ad real terrorist?
The East or the Europeans,
Who used to lie, teef and kill?
Civilizing human beings

Who used to chop of heads?
Stretch short man mek dem tall,
An when dem dun wid dem wickedness
Ah God name dem wan call

Who tek we outta Africa?
Cram we inna dem ships,
Sail we all across da world
Buss we arse wid chains and whips

Who ah sit back while people ah starve?
While dem ah dash way so much feast,
Drain de whole ah Africa
Den garn inna da Middle East

Who start war among da neighbours?
Den gi dem da bombs and tanks,
Ah who ago safe da people dem?
Of coarse dem same dutty yanks

Fool da world wid dem propaganda
Da weapons garn a miss,
Dem wan you to watch da Muslim dem
But who ah da real Terrorist?

MISSING

Left from where she once dwelled
Missing
Gone from the streets,
Love has rebelled

In the hearts of man
No longer,
Taken by envy and greed
Missing
In a far away land
Painfully she bleeds

Knock
But love don't live here,
Conscience has left her side
Missing
From our leaders
Has love just simply died?

Will peace prevail?
When love has gone
Missing
From a song,
When hatred is so powerful
Will love keep holding on?

FROM WHERE WE CAME

We came from great warriors
From lands with soils so rich,
Powerful
With the knowledge to build
To the greatest heights
Long before the time of bricks

Our bodies draped in gold
The sun reflecting from our unblemished skins,
Royalty
Glowing from every wall
Standing tall
Great Queens and Kings

Years have passed, now modern times
Did we remember our pass?
Forgotten
Walking with solemn faces
Like black is a lower class

Many before us stood so firm
Took the shackle from the chain,
Garvey, X and Luther King
Fredrick Douglas,
A few of many, who took the reigns
So that slavery did not remain

Do they rest in peace?
While we fight for material claims,
Hopeless
Like long lost souls,
Did we forget
From where we came?

YES! PRIME MINISTER

Education! Education! Education!
Ya too damn lie,
Our kids are failing in dis system
How can u trust dis grey suit bwoy?

Can u really see wha gwaan?
When u standing behind one bush,
Gone ah Iraq pon a quick ting
Shoulda known dem Muslim stush

Kill we wid ya taxes
Ya soon tax da air we breathe,
All me hear is "Hear! Hear! Hear!
I'm listening ya lickle teef

Politics or pure politricks
U ah tek big man fe fool,
Ya nah dip inna ya pocket
Ah Lord Harris ah build all de school

So wha ya ah do wid we money
Me nah see no hospital ward
An every rarted ting a go up,
Imagine! drive me car an get charge

Now nuttin nah ease up
An life ah get more sinister
But still u aspect we all fe bow
An bawl, Yes! Prime Minister.

STEP UP YA GAME

I don't want to hear about designer tags
Big man like you,
Your lame arse story about riches from rags
Still walking in a crew

Your mind is shallow like puddles
No purpose to your movements,
Do you feel the pain of a black mans struggles?
At least show some improvement

Ask yourself do you fit that picture
A missing dad, a player, a thug,
A description straight from the English scripture
Do you look in the mirror and show some love?

Why are you walking the street with boys?
Are you teaching them to hustle?
Or are you showing them the way the truth?
How to use their brain as muscles.

Is that money stash legit?
Are you still juggling with no shame?
Or are you planning to be an icon
And stepping up your game

OWN YOUR BEAUTY

So far from European
Revel in your beauty,
Your natural hair
A mark of your true roots
A Nubian Queen, absolutely!

Never deny your darkness,
Don't fade away
The richness of your complexion,
Your sculptured looks
A master piece,
The queen of resurrection

Stay far from exploitation
Your body is a temple
Flaunt your tones
In powerful ways
They fear your true potential

EVIL MIST

There's an evil mist
Hovering over these London streets,
Like fog lingering over a river
Seeping into the veins of man
The snake decides to slither

Mist is on the corner
Lurking in the darkest alleys,
The wolves are hunting in usual packs
Fear is gaining strength
In the distance the sound of guns clap

A mother is running scared
Sons drawing blades like playing cards,
But there are more than fifty two choices
The mist has now turned red
The mind is hearing voices

Murder in the borough
The mist has left the scene,
A youth sleeps in silent slumber
No blood is on his conscience
The dead is just a number.

OPPORTUNITY KNOCKS

Opportunity surrounds you
Like carnival crowds,
But that's long
Maybe you just want to burn a head
Turn up the music loud

Mum don't want you being idle
Everyday is a migraine,
Bills slamming the doormat
Like hail stones,
But you're busy playing games

A college is big and broad on the corner
You pass the library
Everyday on the street,
But you've decided this is ghetto
But how ghetto, when everyday you eat

It takes less energy
To create vision,
Than what is takes to deal with drama
Beef will keep you looking back
That's long
Change your position

Slang makes you a foreigner
They won't translate,
You blind them
From the genius
When opportunity awaits.

FORGET YOUR PASS

Pass tries to sneak up on you
Like poison ivy,
Winding around your destiny
Blocking out your hopeful vision
Until life has no beauty

Pass wants you to remember
When you were crawling,
Down in the natural dirt
You were searching for hope
Helplessly you were falling

Pass is playing mind games
Embedded in your every thought
Violating you
Like an unwanted germ
Every so often he is caught

Pass plays dirty
Attacks you when you're low,
But everyday there is daylight
An every season flowers grow
Life is breathing
So you give back every blow

Pass is still trying
Many sleepless nights in bed,
But notice
He always comes from behind
So simply look ahead.

YEAH BLOOD!

Yeah blood!
You say it so freely
But blood is thicker than water
Yet so easily you take your bredrins life
The only blood I see is slaughter.

HEAR! HEAR! HEAR!

What this thing called politics?
Grey men with a box of tricks,
For them life is grey
Sitting down in the commons all day

Hear! Hear! Hear!
Another bright idea
Speeches read from scripts
Promises of affordable houses
While war is getting ships

Programmed with mechanical smiles
Every move is fake,
Our cups are running over
We're drowning in your taxing lake,
On payday you're like highway thieves
Weapons of mass extortion,
Leave just enough to pay them bills
Credits cards are used with caution

Hear! Hear! Hear!
Another bright idea
More speeches read from scripts
"Lets get tough on crime"
People murdering just for kicks

You said more aid for Africa
But who robbed them dry?
And still I see them starving
Suffer the children
Hear them cry,

Cost of living rising
Wages stay the same
Caught up in this matrix
Always going against the grain

Hear! Hear! Hear!
That familiar sound
But who's caring for the people
The divide between rich and poor
Surely can't be legal

MY YOUT

I see no bad boy in you
Just a lost sheep
Following the street dog
But he has no sense
No plan
His mind is lost in the fog

My guidance could have saved you
I've seen the wounds
Witnessed many scars,
Seen men die
Ones I grew with
Others call from behind bars

You rejected my words
Like as if they were poison,
I gave you signs to follow
Instead you tried to test me
I could have sparked you
But I'll leave you for the streets to swallow

I know I'm not your blood
But I took you
Just like my own,
Tried to teach you manhood
The road is not your oyster
But you decided to go it alone

THE ENDZ

Is it your endz?
These streets
These miles and miles of concrete,
You say you're minding your manor
But you have no manners
Life is more than a heartbeat

That youth was passing through
His thoughts on home,
His mind already on feather filled pillows
You could have left him alone,
But it your endz

You and the boys in unseen zones
Weed flowing through flared noses,
I kind of street romance
But there are more guns than roses

That youth was passing through
Now surrounded by shallow urges,
Hood rats have him scoped
No Christian
But now he's reciting verses

Frightened like pray to a lion
His hands up like shields,
You devour him like your life depends
Sharp blades turn red,
He falls helplessly
Dying for the endz.

I'M A CELEBRITY

I see your skinny arse on glossy magazines,
I mistook you
For the staple between the pages
Like your shit don't stink,
What! You've bought a new handbag
Go and eat some food
That's what I think

Your more plastic than Barbie doll
Stay away from the Caribbean sands,
That might melt your backside
You should have left it flat
And saved yourself some grand's

I pass you on the street
You're no more special
Than fried rice,
Sometimes I don't recognise you
Until you've topped up your tan
And your breast keep growing in size

You're as real as a waxwork dummy
Your heart
Green, just like money
You throw it freely on coke lines,
Get a sniff of poverty
No, you'd probably have a breakdown
Have to sell your body parts
Then try and hold your head high
Around town

Your dog dresses better than I do
His kennel's bigger
Than my yard
Taking him hairdressers
What kind of shit is that?
And buying him a birthday card,
Yeah I know you're a celebrity
Every time I buy a paper
I see your mug,
I don't business about your
Third husband
Third divorce
Third house
And third horse

Would you give to a homeless man?
Maybe buy him a coffee,
No, you wouldn't stoop that low
Probably pass him by
Leave him to die
Then go and spend a million on a brand new toe.

LETS PRAY

Our Father, who walks with me on these crooked paths
Guide me away from open holes,
So that if I may fall
On myself, the blame will pass

Bless them who try turning me into ruins
For their words are weak,
And if they put force upon me
I will never turn the other cheek

Protect my girl child from the preying beast
Who finds pleasure in children's innocence,
For I will be responsible for my actions
And I would wilfully go behind the prison fence

Thank you for the food that replenishes my body
For every day that I breathe,
And I am truly grateful
For the will in me to achieve,

Show these youths that life is precious
Open their eyes for them to see,
Teach them to listen to the wise
And that wisdom is the key

Let them leaders know that you are watching them
For they suffer us with their wicked ways,
Still I will remain the same
The lion in me will never stray

I give thanks for the mother that birth me
For putting morals in my blend,
I thank you for the person that I am
For you are the almighty… Amen!

COMMENTS

All comments and feedback on this book will be most appreciated
Send emails to: deepboy371@yahoo.co.uk

FOR FRAMED POETRY

ANY OCCASION OR SUBJECT COVERED

PERSONALISED TO THE INDIVIDUAL

EMAIL OR CALL ME ON

07958 356 071